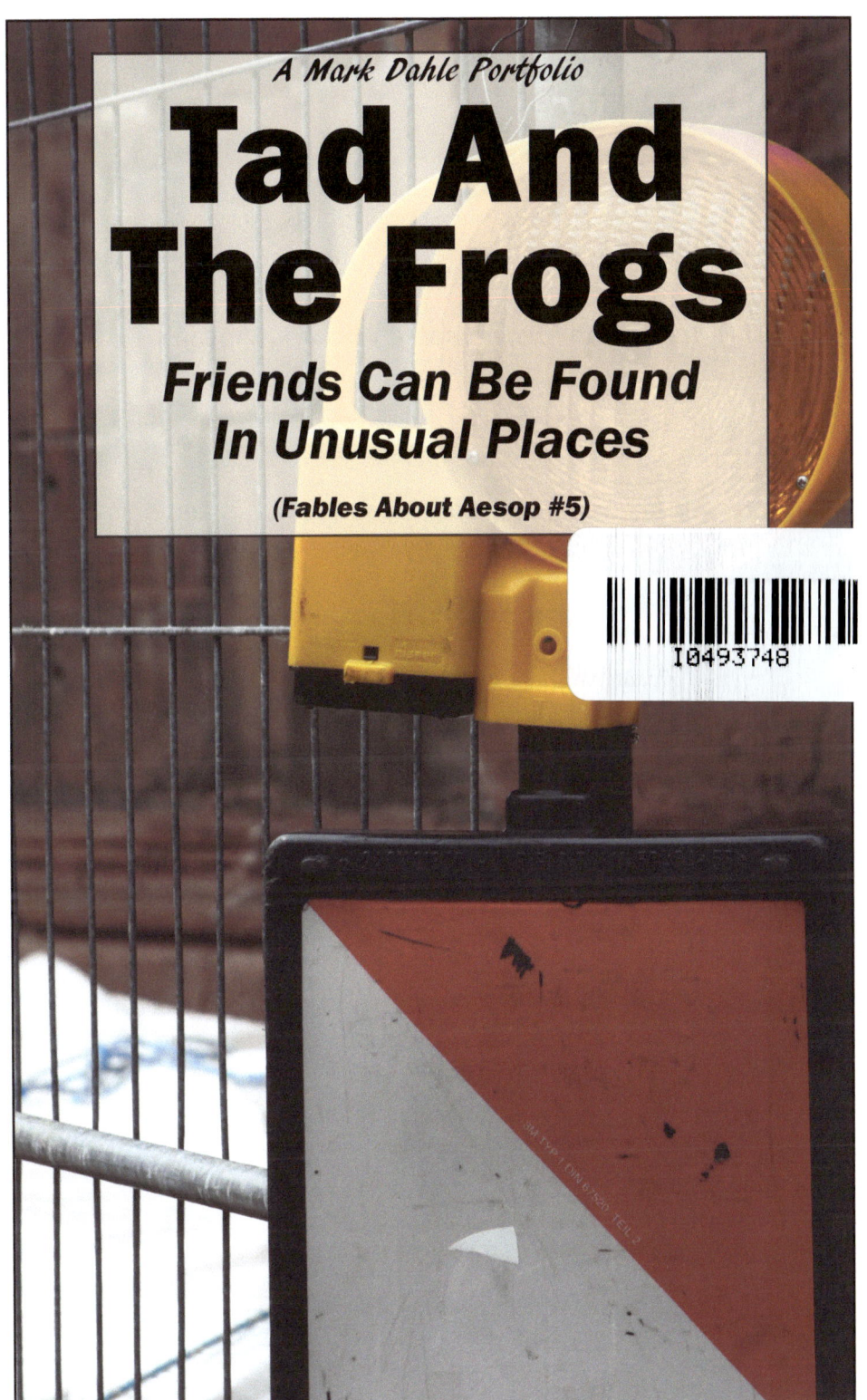

A Mark Dahle Portfolio

Tad And The Frogs

Friends Can Be Found In Unusual Places

(Fables About Aesop #5)

Mark Dahle has written many great fables about Aesop.
This is #5.

~ ~ ~

Mark Dahle Portfolios can be read in a few minutes and enjoyed
for a lifetime.

Unlike many picture books, the text is not related to the beautiful
painting at the right and the photographs that follow. This might
seem a little weird at first. One thing that helps is to order more
portfolios until you get used to it. In the meantime, feel free to
draw your own pictures of Aesop if you like.

This portfolio includes a photo of a brilliant 36 x 24 inch painting
(at the right), twenty-five beautiful pictures from Freiburg,
Germany and Hawaii, and a story about Aesop making some
unusual friends.

Photographs in this book are available in very limited editions.
See http://www.MarkDahle.com for more information and for
previews of upcoming portfolios.

We do our best to create portfolios free of editing mistakes. But it's hard to
catch everything. We reward people who report errors in any Mark Dahle
portfolio. For details see MarkDahle.com/Typos.html or send an email to
MarkDahle@aol.com with the subject line "Typos." Thanks!

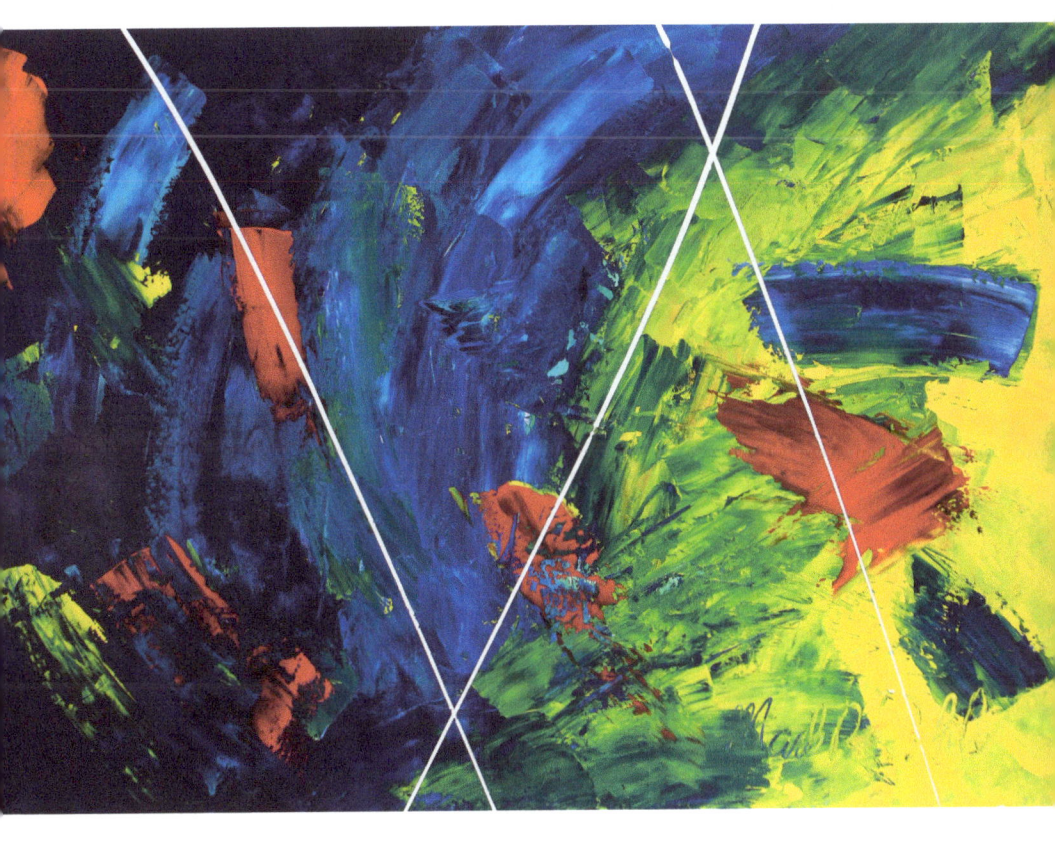

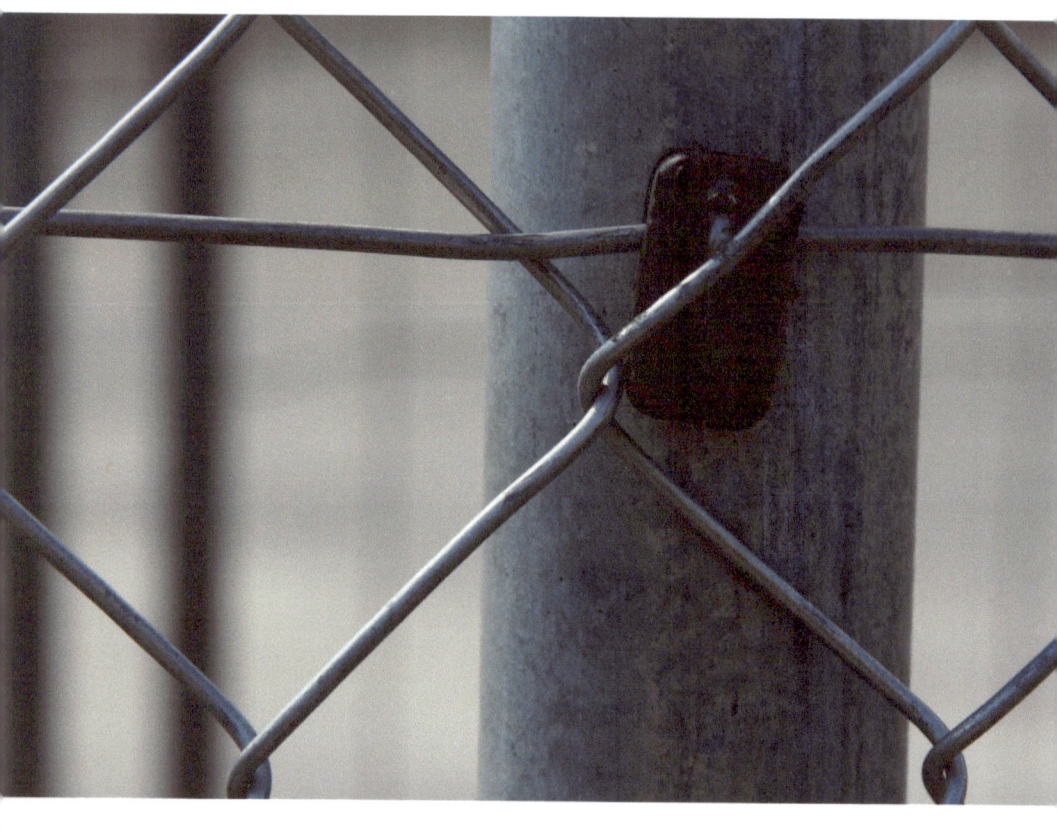

Octavia held Tad's shirt. Tad had written "I'm with Aesop" in big letters on the front.

"What does *that* mean?" she asked.

"I don't know," Aesop said. "He's part of a gang that beats me up."

Octavia looked at her son. It was the first time he'd mentioned it.

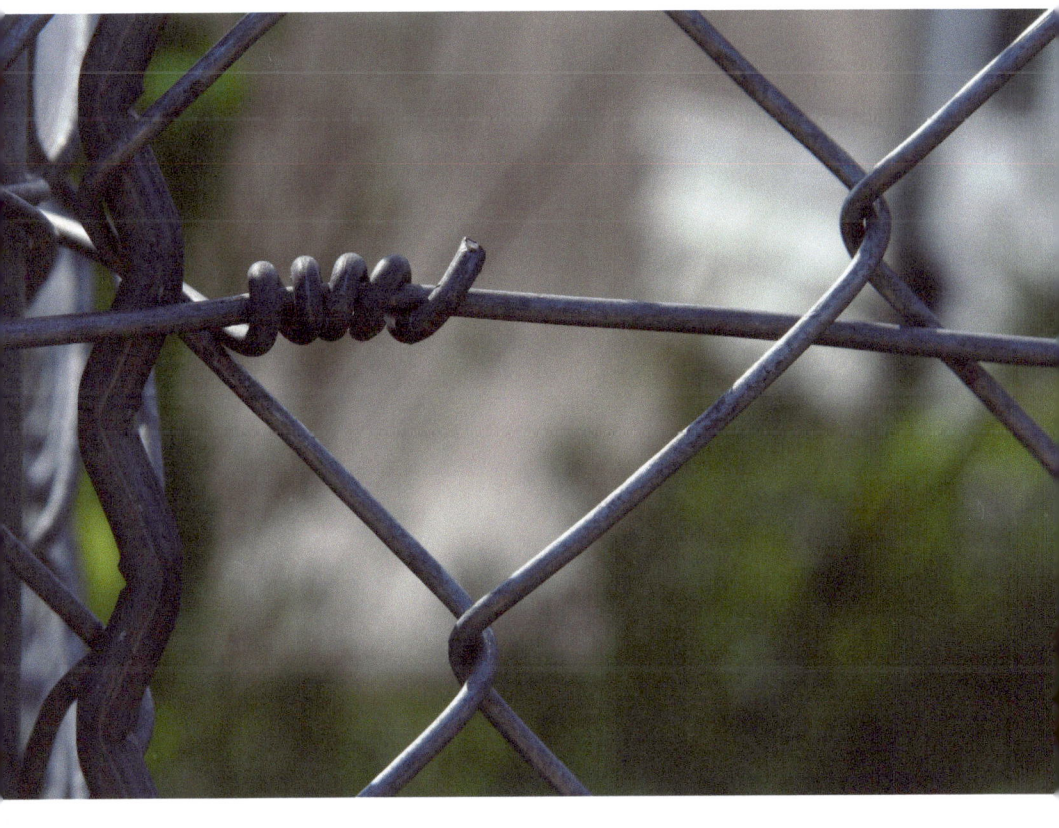

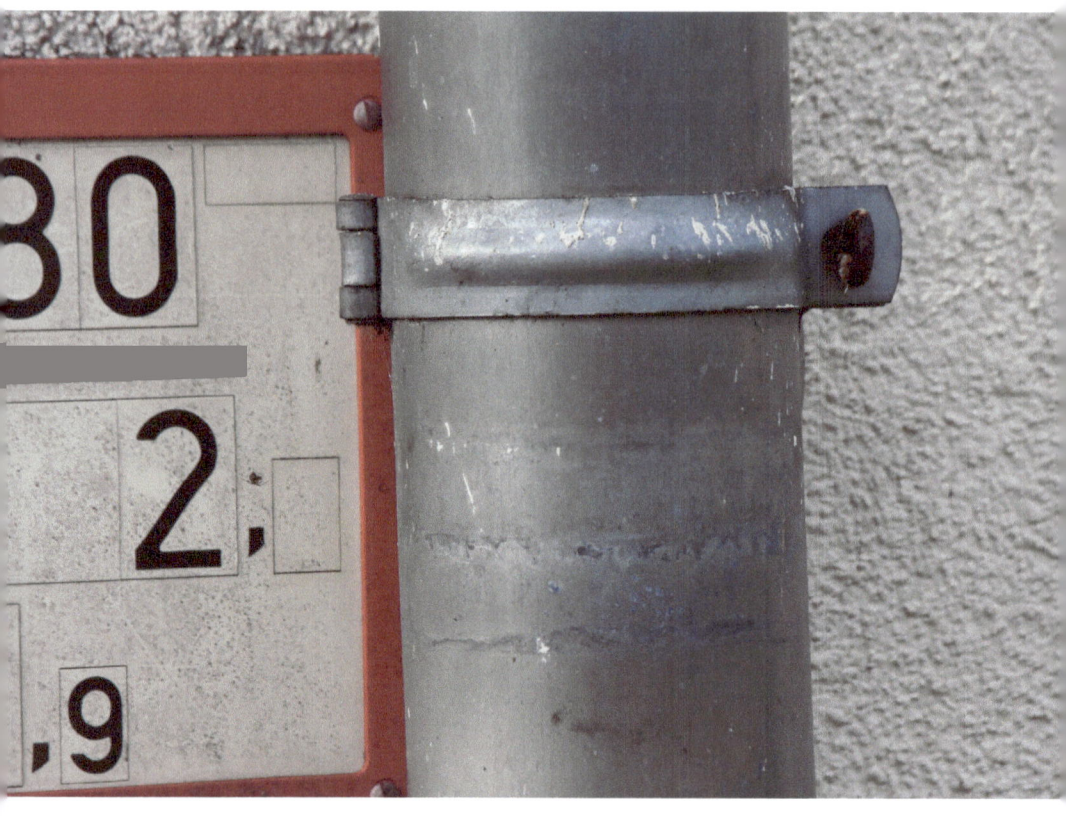

"Well," she said, "it looks like he changed his mind for some reason. We'll have to go see the guards again."

They walked in silence to the guard station.

When they arrived, Jurek was on duty. Jurek had questioned Hektor about Tad's death. Hektor had said Tad ruined a shirt by writing some gibberish on it, but Hektor hadn't mentioned what the writing said.

"Why do you think Tad wrote this?" Jurek asked Aesop.

"I don't know," Aesop said. "I thought he didn't like me."

"Did anything happen to change that?"

Aesop looked down at his feet.

"You can tell me, Aesop," Jurek said.

"I told him frogs would bring him luck."

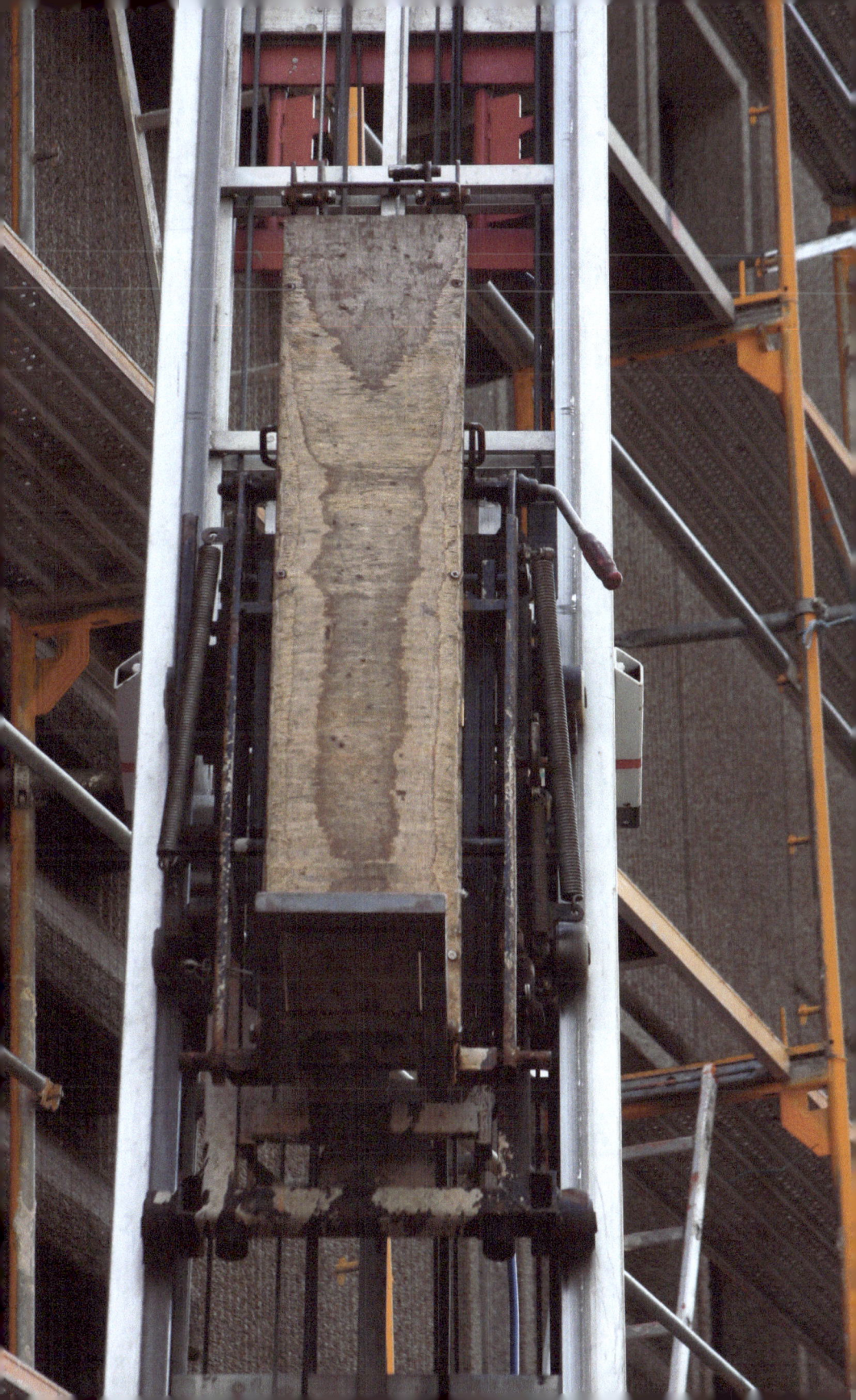

Dachde

Peter Schweizer
7815 Kirchzarten

21

Jurek waited patiently. Soon the whole story came tumbling out: why Aesop had said that and how Tad started spending time in the swamp after he heard he could find luck there. How Aesop thought Tad's death might be his fault. How Aesop was planning to not tell any more stories because he didn't want any more people to be hurt.

"Tad's death wasn't your fault, Aesop," Jurek said gently. He sighed. "It looks like we'll need to investigate some more. If we find anything either of you should know, we'll get back to you."

Damian was called out of school that day. He appeared confident until he saw the guard's uniform. Then his face lost some of its color.

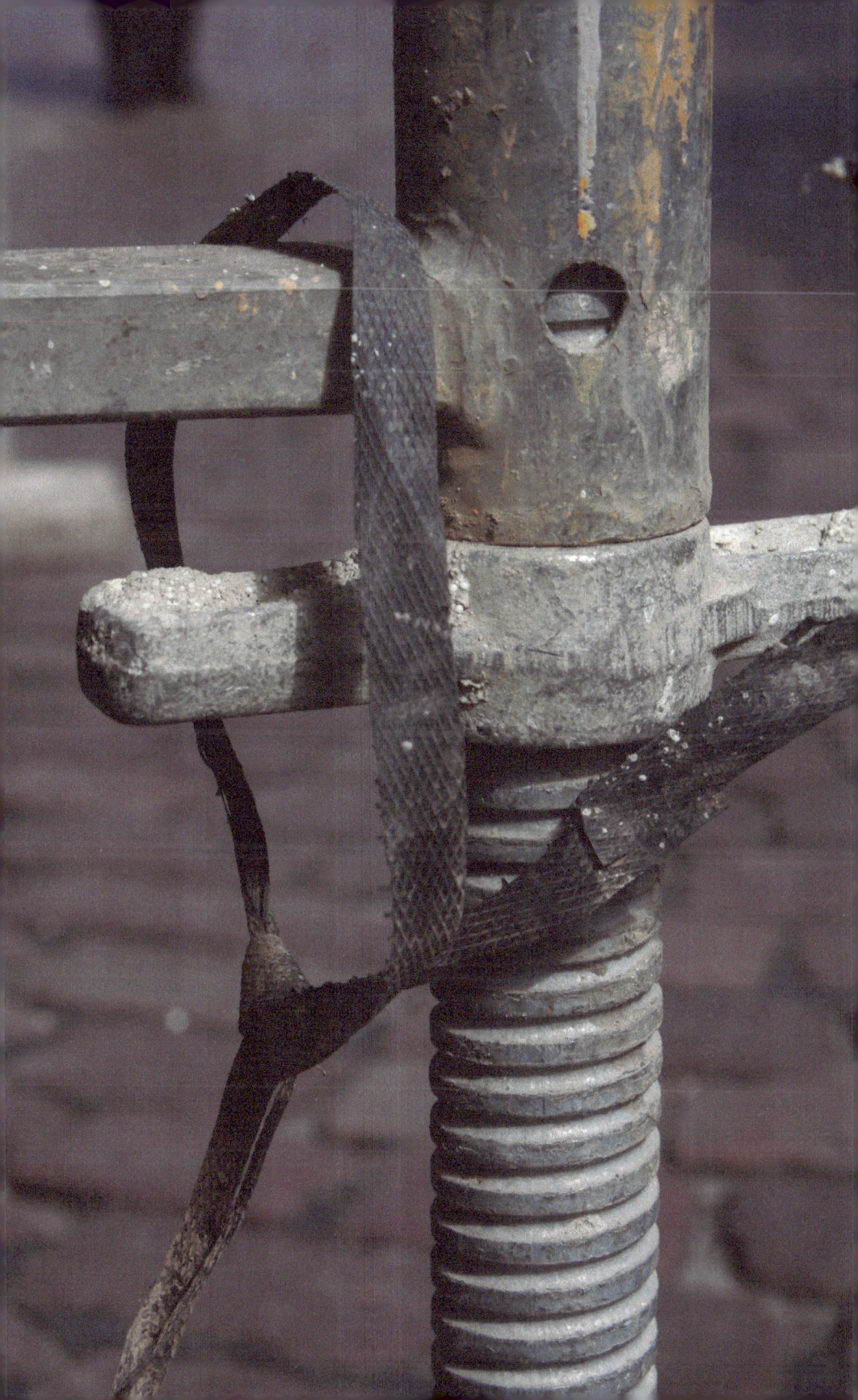

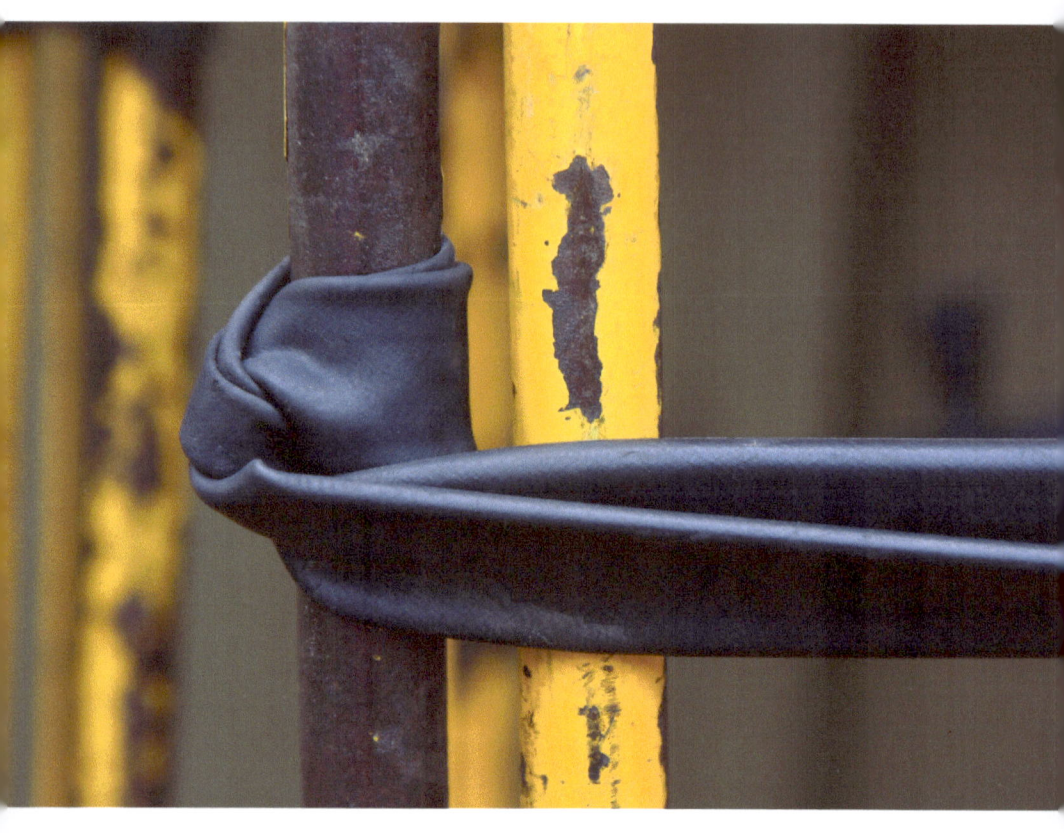

"It's not my fault," he said.

"What's that?" asked Jurek.

"I told Mr. Garis where to find Tad. I didn't know he'd kill him." A tear rolled down his face, but his mouth was set in a tight line and he was determined not to break down.

Jurek had a son Damian's age. He had practice sitting patiently and creating the right openings to hear the details of his son's life. Now he listened to Damian until he heard the whole story.

The day Tad had died, Damian had skipped a morning class to take some food to him. He had tried to get him to leave the swamp.

"Frogs don't give you luck," he had said.

"You're as lucky as you think you are," Tad said.

"And if I don't think I'm lucky?"

"Then things will go better for you as soon as you change your mind."

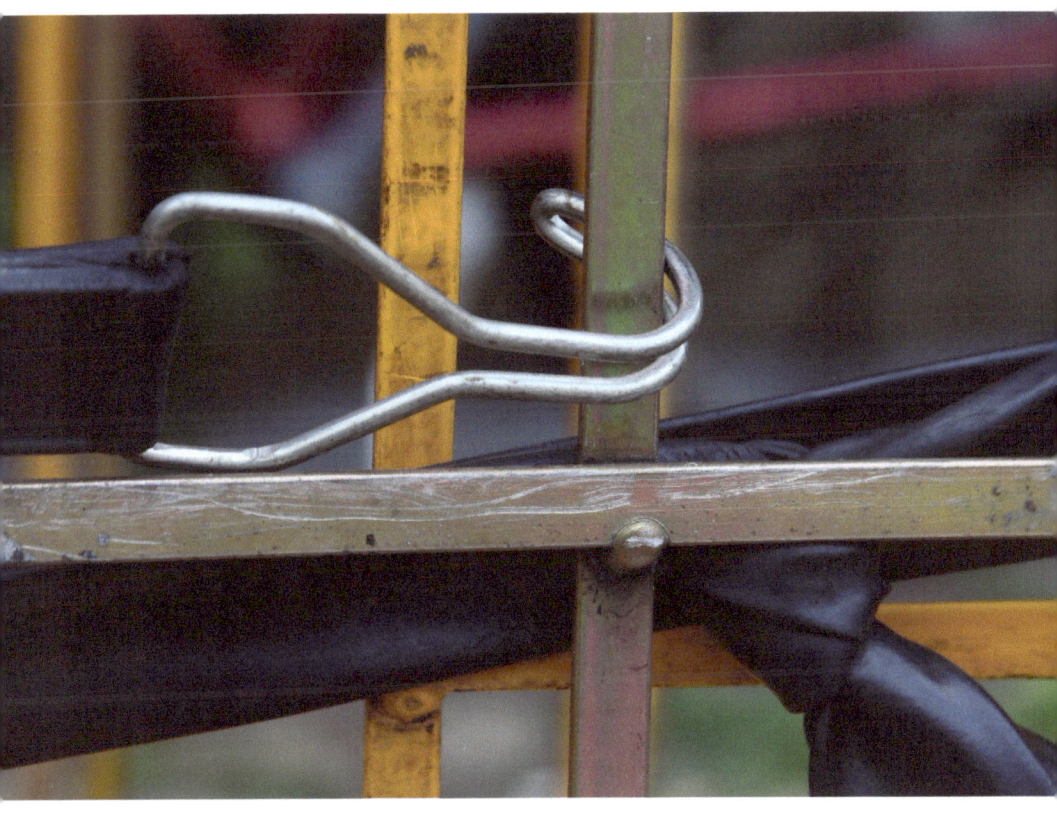

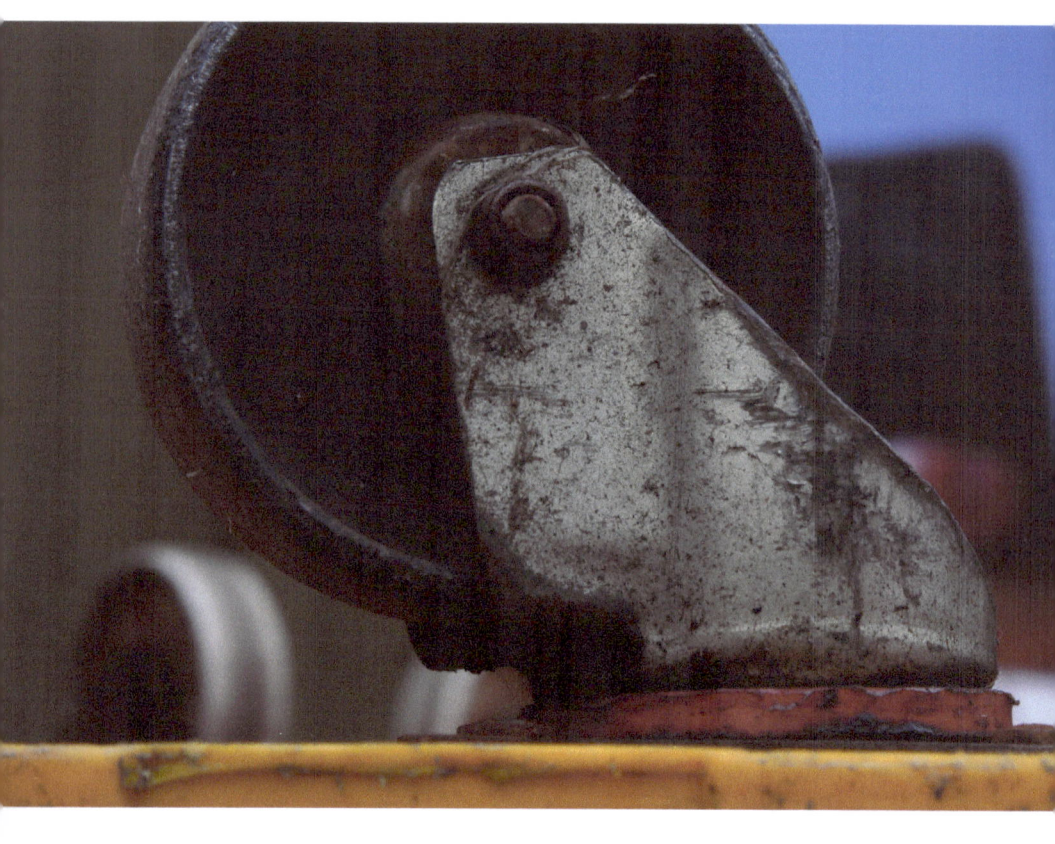

Damian had considered this. He would have liked for things to go better in his life. But he could not get over the evidence before him. "How about you?" he said. "You're not lucky."

"Oh, I don't know," Tad had said. "I'm lucky enough. I quit hating Aesop."

"What's *that* got to do with it?"

"Until this week I was afraid every night when my dad came home. Had he been at the Broken Wheel? Would he be mad about something? Would I get hurt?

"But this week? This week I'm not afraid. A week ago, I didn't think I'd be alive today. But here I am. The frogs are giving me luck."

Damian looked away.

"Look," Tad said. "Living in the swamp has drawbacks. I don't get to see you and Javan so much. I'm hungry, more than normal. But it's beautiful here. I didn't know that before." He paused. "Aesop helped me see that. He's not so bad. He's just trying to get by like the rest of us."

"You better not let Javan hear you say that."

"Javan will have to get used to it," Tad said. "I'm going to live with Aesop. His mom is working something out. I'll only be in the swamp a couple more days."

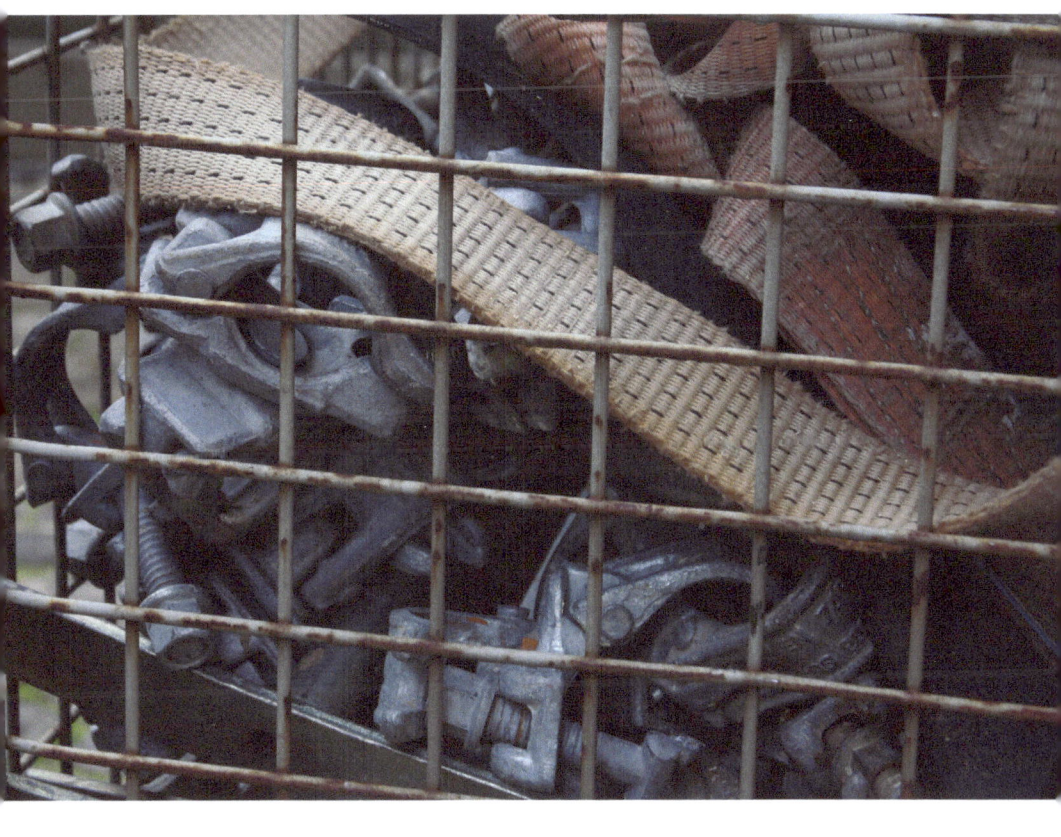

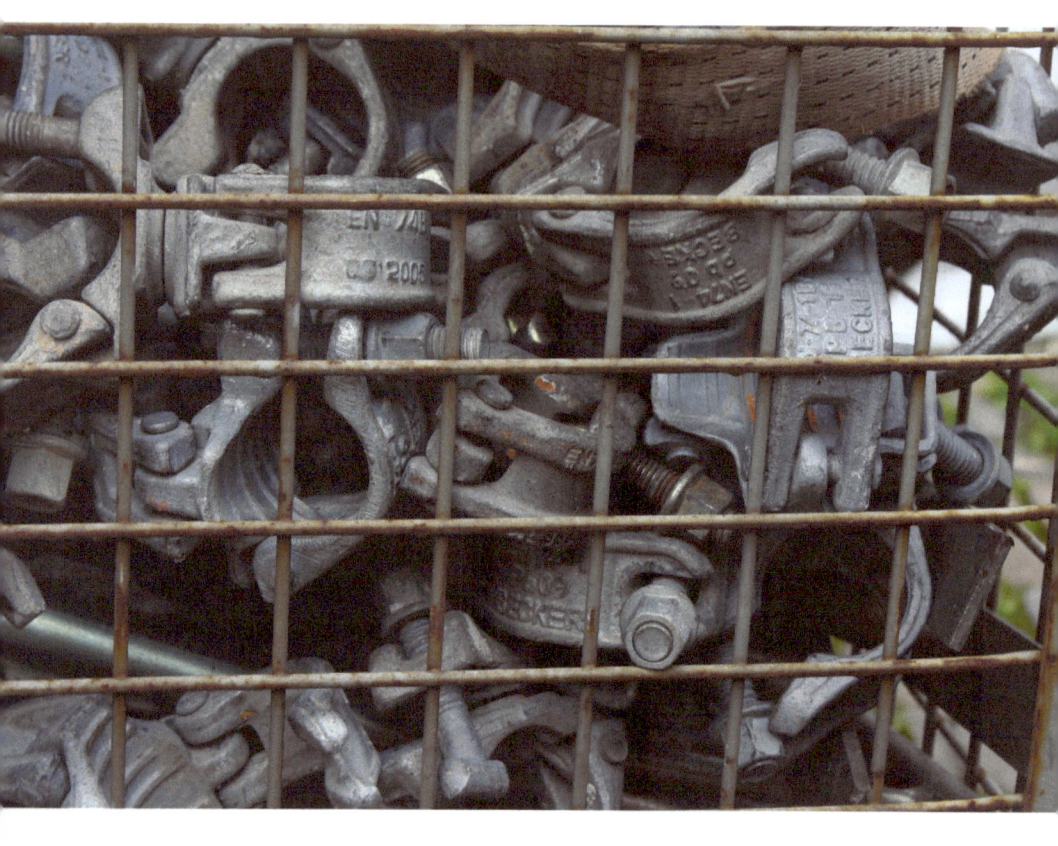

When Octavia heard Tad's plan a short while later, she had been startled and then she started to cry. She hadn't realized how much Tad was counting on her to create the change he had sought. It wouldn't have happened as fast as Tad was expecting.

The only other thing of note in Damian's interview happened when they showed him Tad's shirt. "It didn't have any writing on it when I saw him," Tad said.

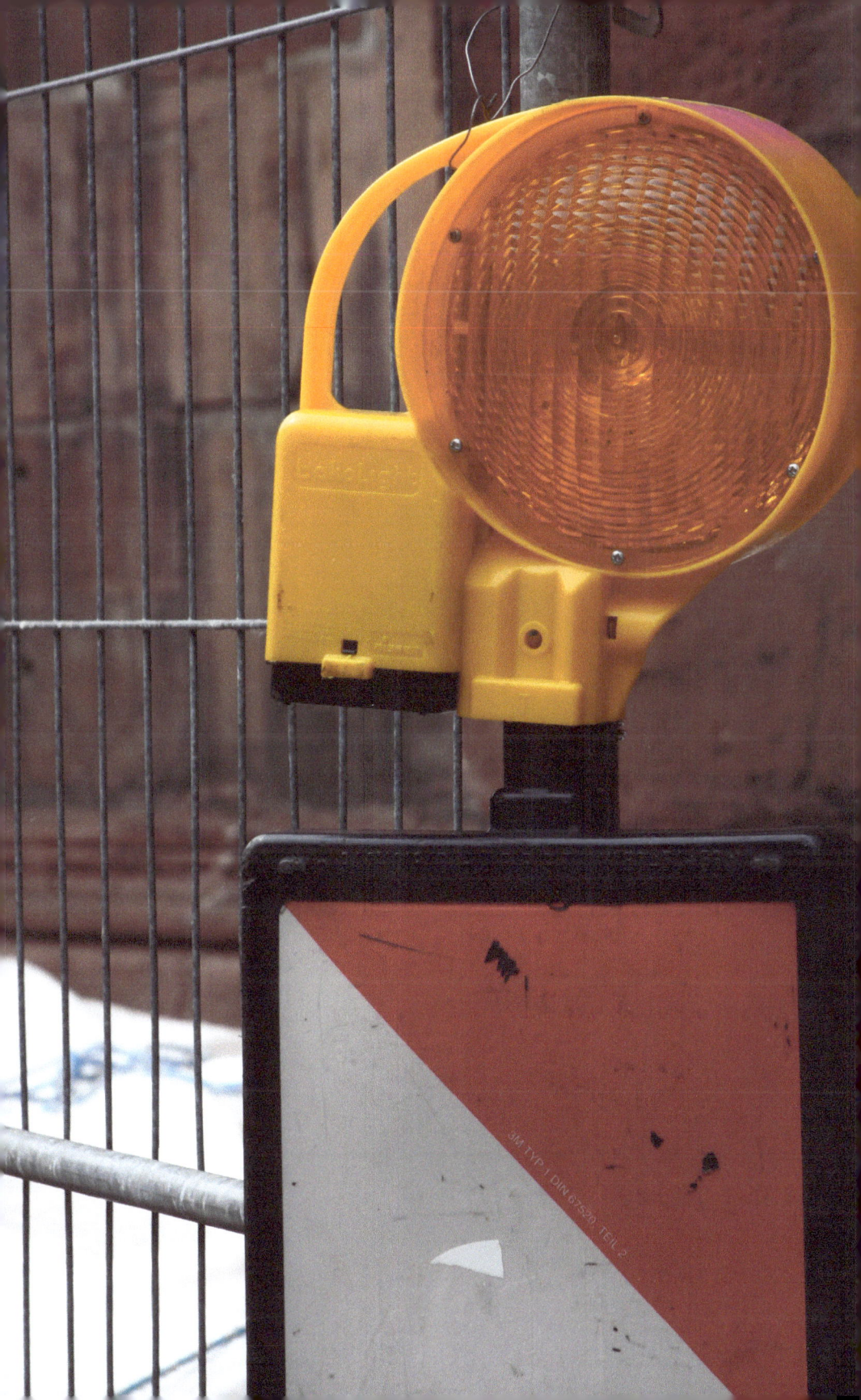

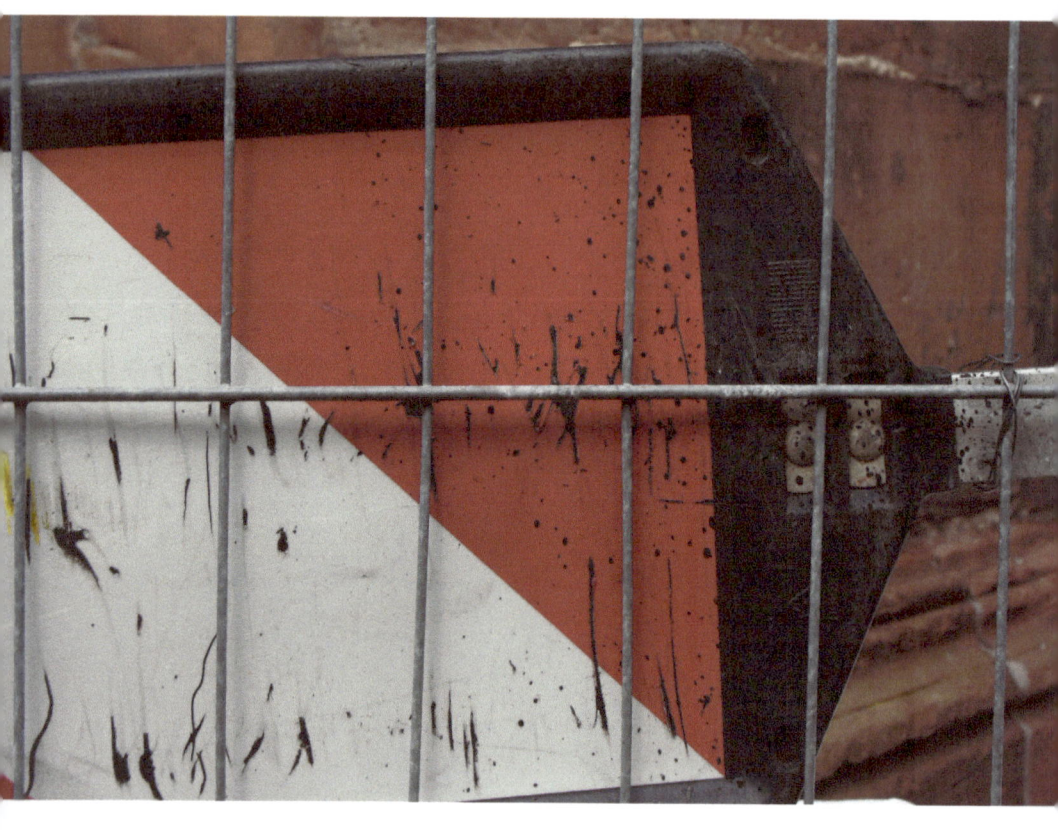

A little later when Javan was interviewed, he didn't believe it when he was told of Tad's plans to live with Aesop. "No way," he had said. At last they showed him Tad's shirt.

Javan quit talking and took a step back. "You just made that up," he said. But he recognized Tad's writing. He wouldn't say anything more after that.

The guards figured that on the day of Tad's death, Damian had seen him, given him food, and left. On his way back to school, Damian had told Tad's dad where Tad was. Before Mr. Garis arrived, Tad had written "I'm with Aesop" on his shirt, probably as a result of his conversation with Damian.

The guards knew the writing had provoked Hektor, but Jurek guessed that Hektor was angry enough to hurt his son even before he saw the shirt. The shirt might not have mattered.

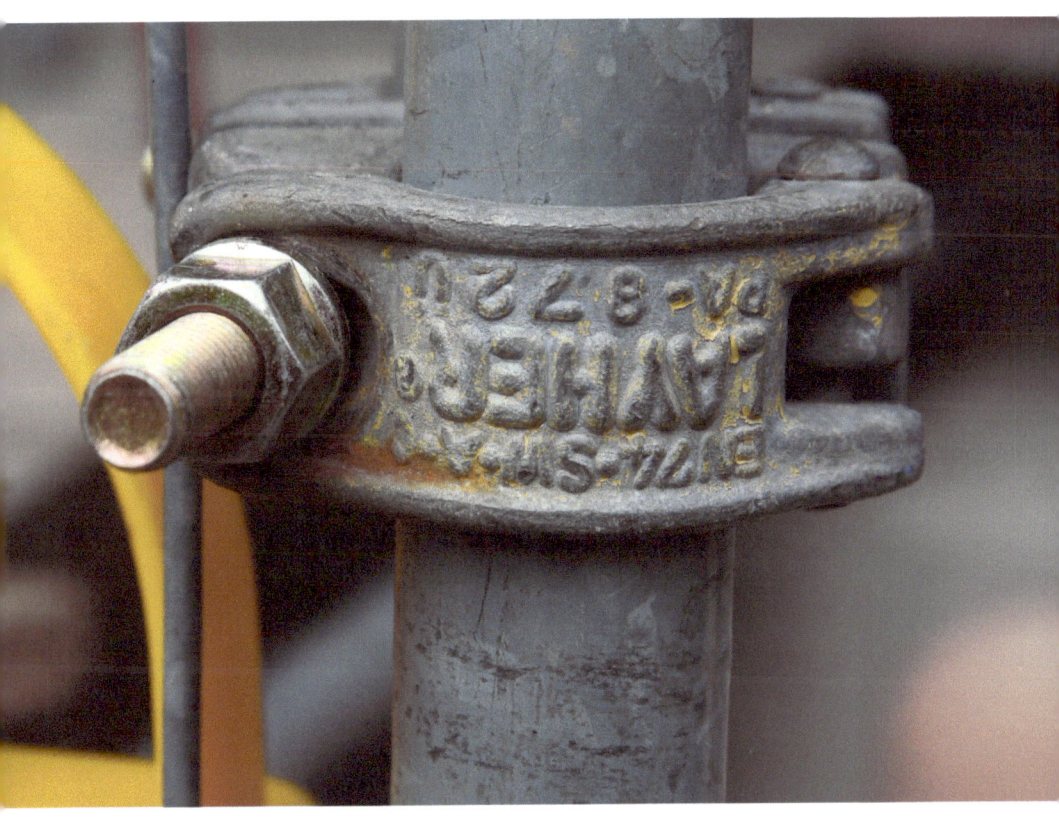

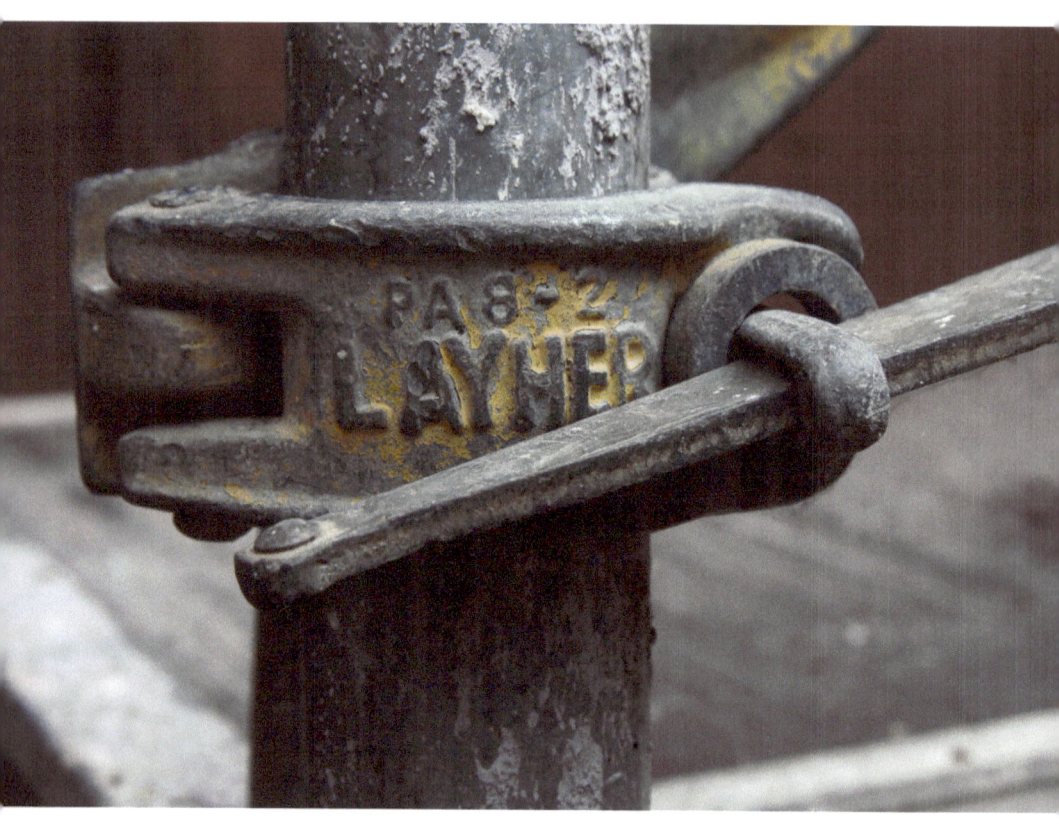

The guards concluded, since most of the blood was on the back of the shirt, that Tad had been hit from behind, maybe with a rock or a board.

The guards couldn't know, since there were no witnesses, that Tad had lived several hours after being hit.

Tad didn't know, when he got up after being hit, how bad his injury was; he thought he was alright. He was a little light headed, but he was fine. In fact, he was deliriously happy. In a couple days he would have a new home where his dad wouldn't hit him. Octavia was fixing that up. In the meantime, he was someplace beautiful. He was at home in the swamp.

When Tad finally noticed the blood, he changed shirts, then he continued walking around the swamp, enjoying the day. It was one of Tad's best days ever. He was really enjoying himself, his freedom, the sunshine, the setting. Then he stumbled and fell and didn't get up.

When Tad had been hit, the blow had caused a brain hemorrhage. After the bleeding in his brain reached a tipping point, Tad went from light-headed happiness to unconsciousness in a moment. Soon afterwards he stopped breathing.

Because Tad's father was in jail, it fell to the guards to arrange Tad's burial.

Niilo, Jurek's supervisor, insisted that Tad be buried in the shirt that said "I'm with Aesop." Niilo was deeply superstitious. He hoped the blood on the shirt would get Tad sympathy in the world of the dead and help him to be treated better.

"Plus the writing about Aesop might help," he said. "Perhaps in the world of the dead they have already heard of how Aesop brings luck. Maybe being associated with Aesop will bring Tad luck with the dead."

Other guards rolled their eyes when they heard this, but not everyone. To some it made a lot of sense.

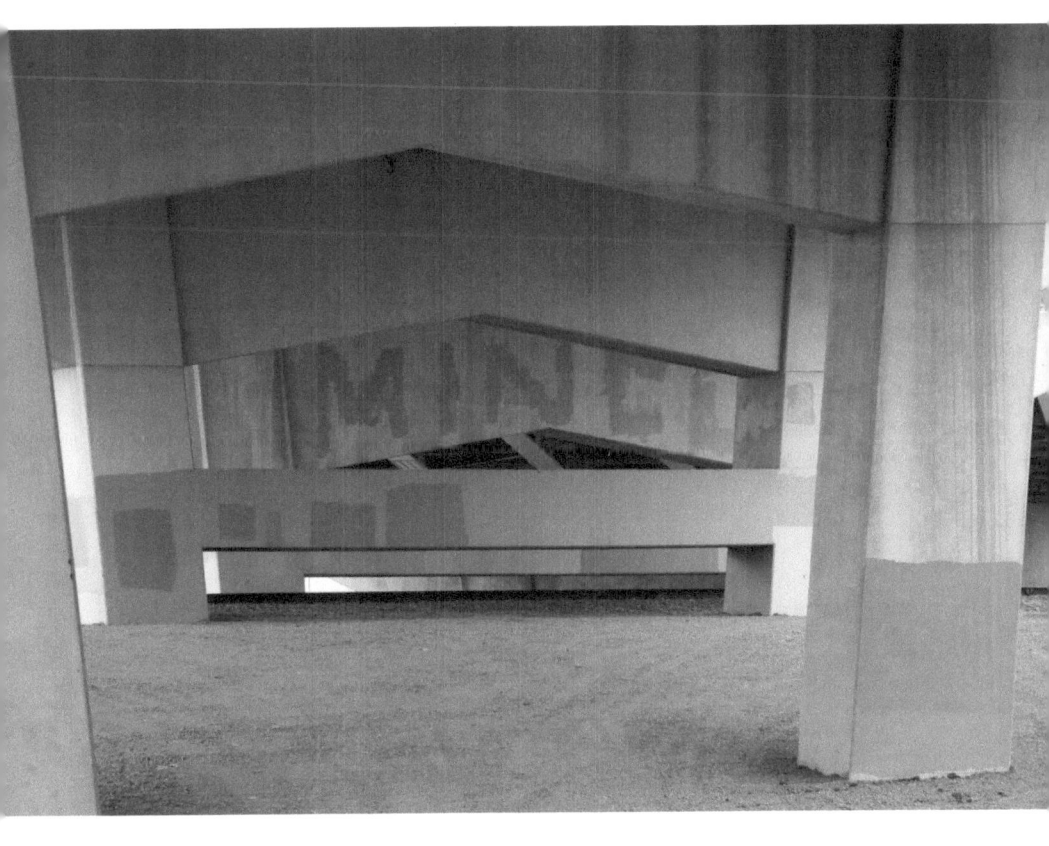

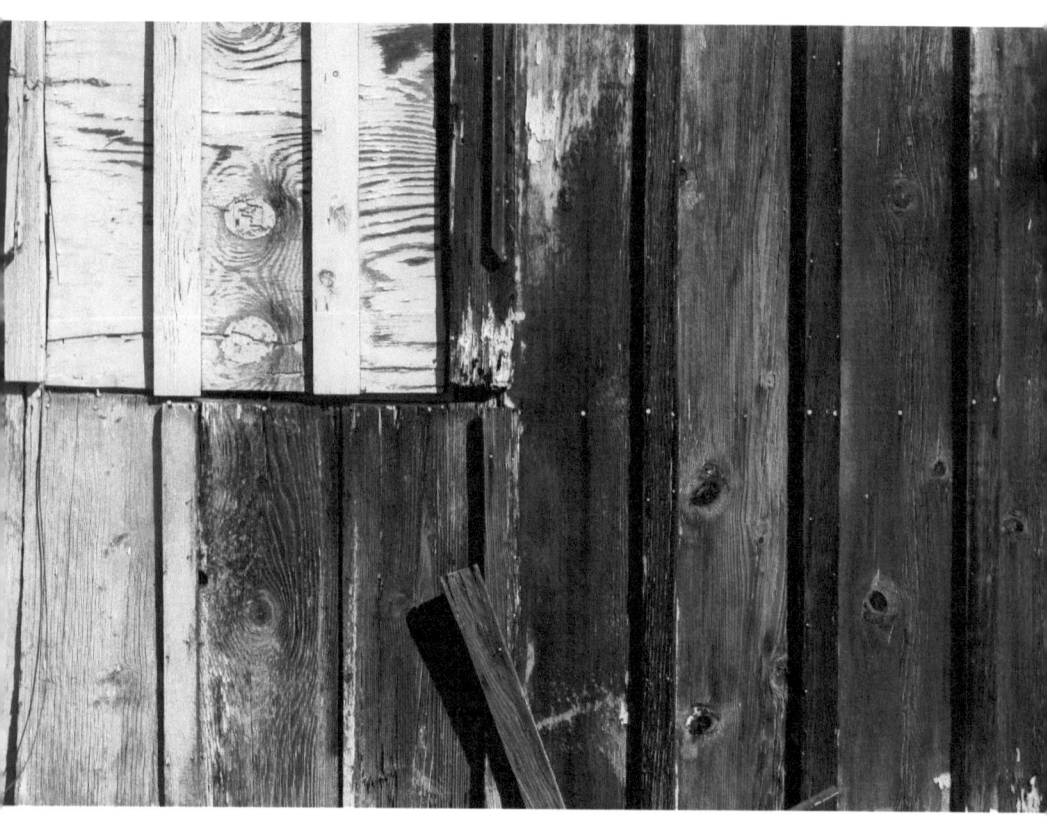

The next day, Tad's body was carried in procession to the graveyard before dawn.

Aesop, Javan and Damian had each been asked to say something before the body was buried.

Javan had refused. "Aesop is the one who should talk," he said. "Get him to tell a story. He's getting better at it."

For his part, Aesop was determined to never tell a story again. He thought his story had probably gotten Tad killed.

"It seems so odd," Aesop said earlier, when Octavia talked to him about the funeral plans. "The only one who's not feeling sad and guilty about all this is Mr. Garis, and he's the one who killed Tad."

Octavia finally convinced Aesop to say something at the funeral in honor of Tad. "Aesop," she said, "Tad had changed. It's too bad you never got to find out how much."

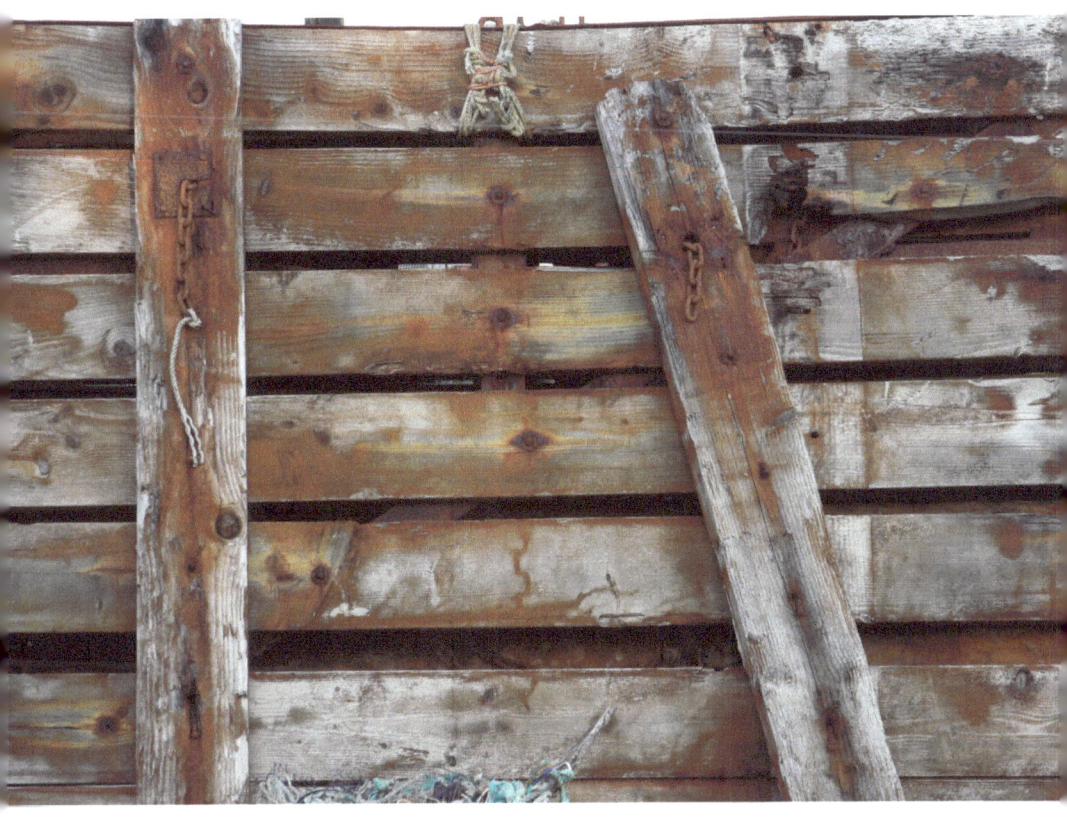

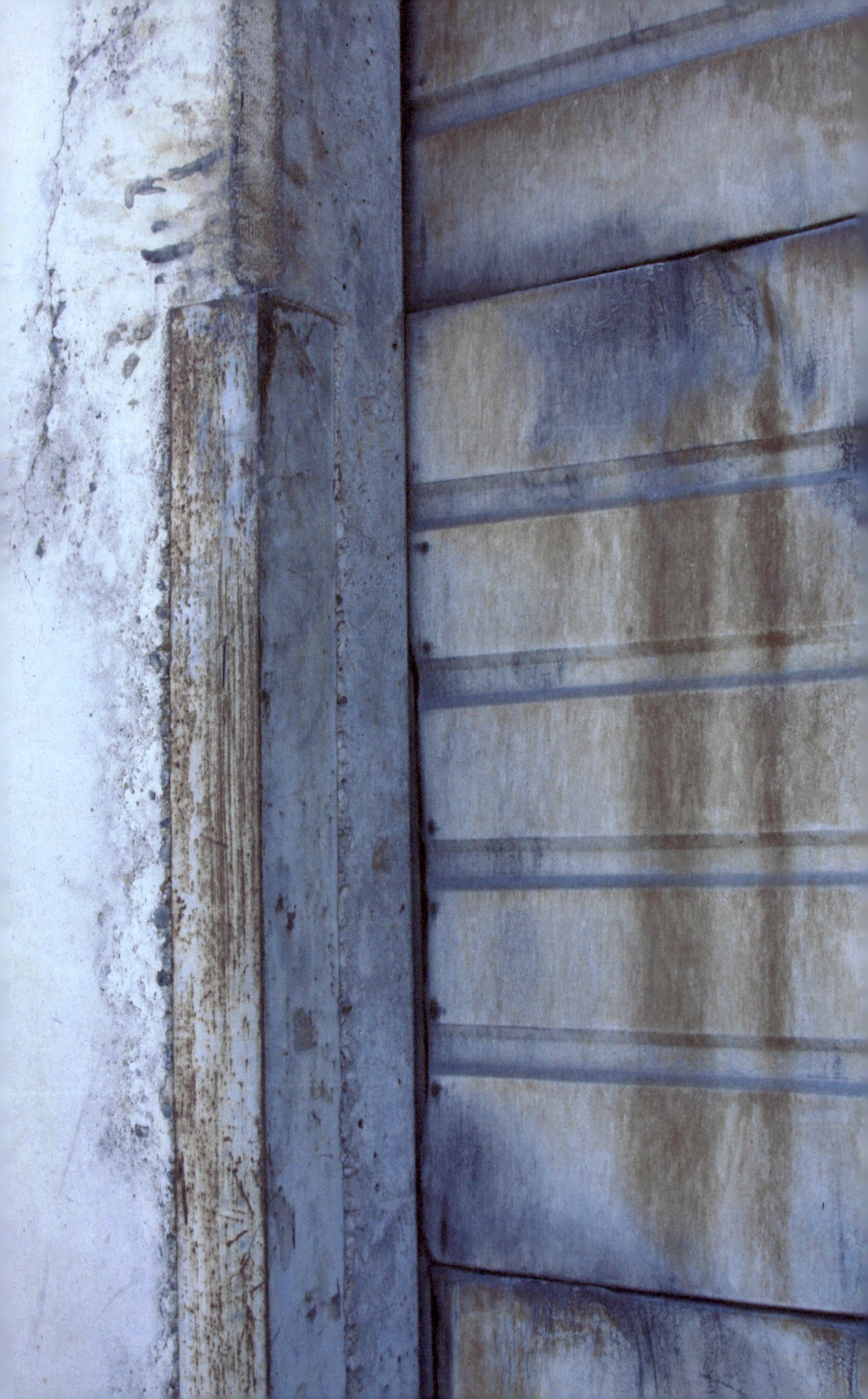

In the end, Aesop was the only one who spoke at Tad's funeral.

When the procession arrived at the gravesite, Aesop cleared his throat and began.

"You never know where you're going to find a friend," Aesop had said. "Friends can be found in unusual places.

"A week ago, Tad came to me with a frog in each hand. He had found them in the swamp. He could have killed them. People sometimes do. But somehow, Tad became a friend to those frogs. I imagine they were surprised. I know I was surprised when Tad became a friend to me.

"The frogs helped Tad notice how beautiful the swamp is. I've heard some people say he was not very lucky because he died. But he was surrounded by beauty he had never noticed before and by new friends. There's nothing unlucky about that."

The next day, when Aesop was on his way to school, he rounded a bend and saw Javan and Damian blocking his path.

Aesop thought about turning around. He thought about running. But then he took a deep breath and walked straight towards them. He expected to get beat up.

To his surprise, when he got close he saw they both had written "I'm with Aesop" in charcoal on their shirts.

"Now what?" he wondered.

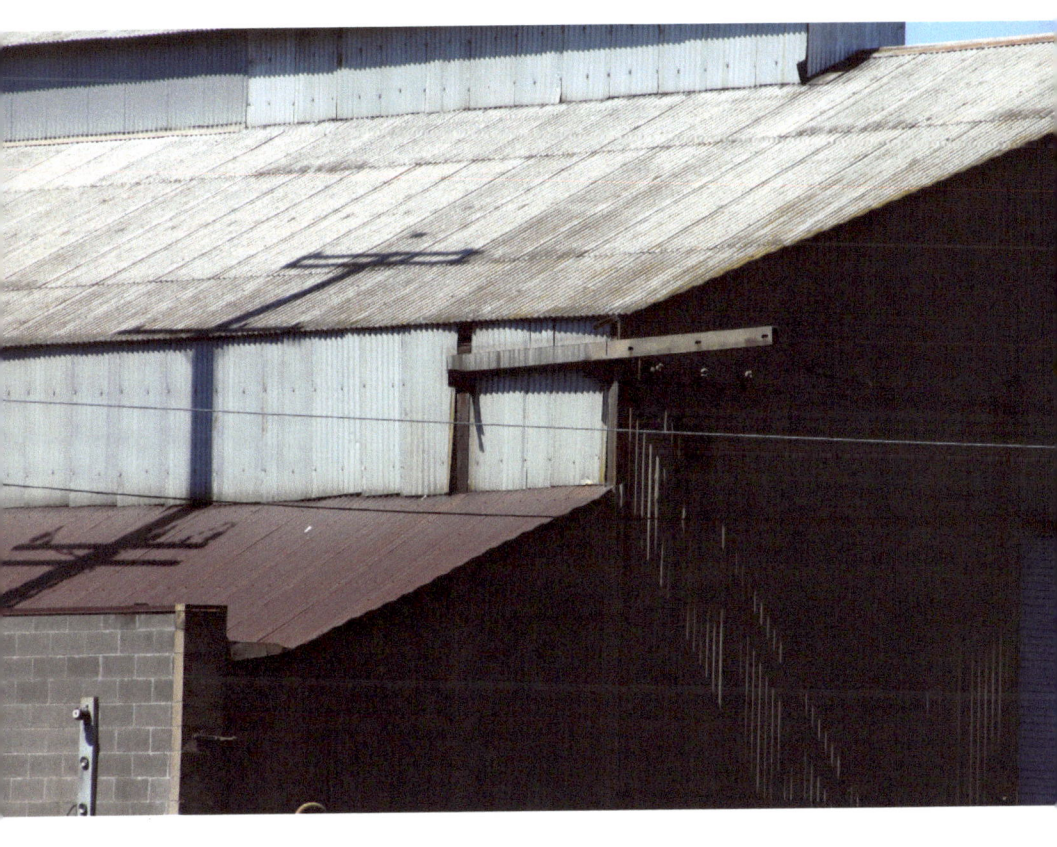

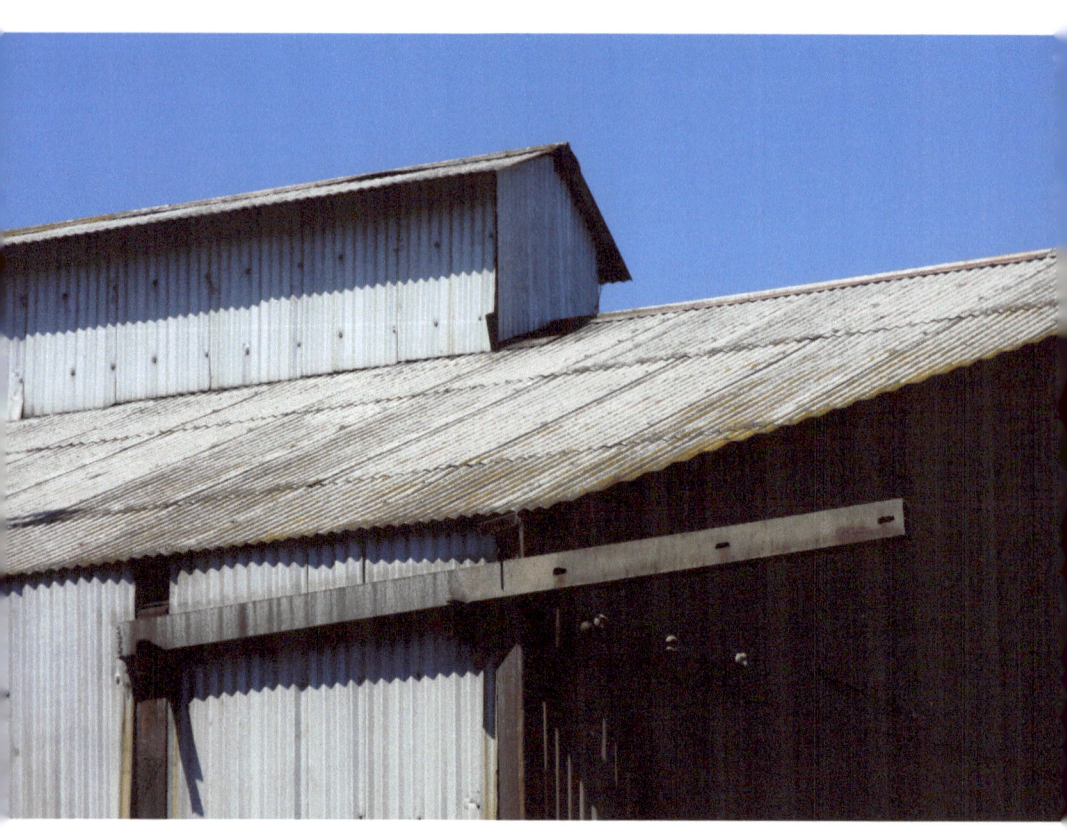

"We've always had three in our gang," Javan said. "Tad said he was with you. Since he can't be in our gang any more, you're taking his place. You don't get a choice. And one thing about being in our gang. No more talk about you not telling any more stories. Monday at lunch you better have one ready. We've never beat up someone *inside* our gang before, and I don't plan to start with you."

At first Aesop didn't react. Then he smiled. If Tad could change, maybe these two could as well.

Maybe they were the friends he'd been hoping for all along. Maybe frogs were lucky after all.

It probably wouldn't be that easy, he thought as he reflected. But you never know. Friends can be found in unusual places.

~~

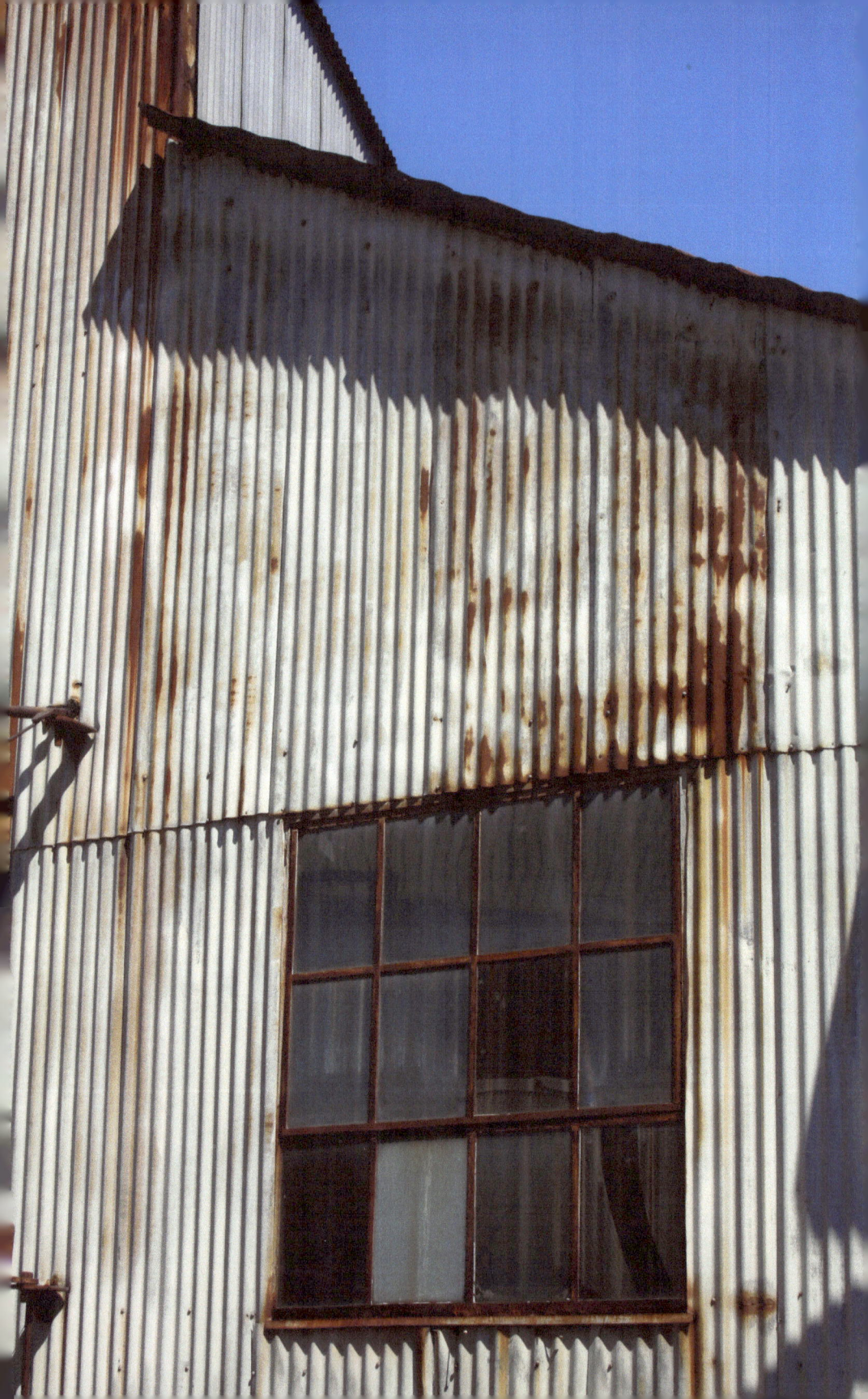

Reflection questions

Who could you be friends with that would be surprising?

What caused Tad to change his mind about Aesop?

What might cause people to change their minds about you?

Tad had never noticed how beautiful the swamp was. What are some places you might explore that you have ignored so far?

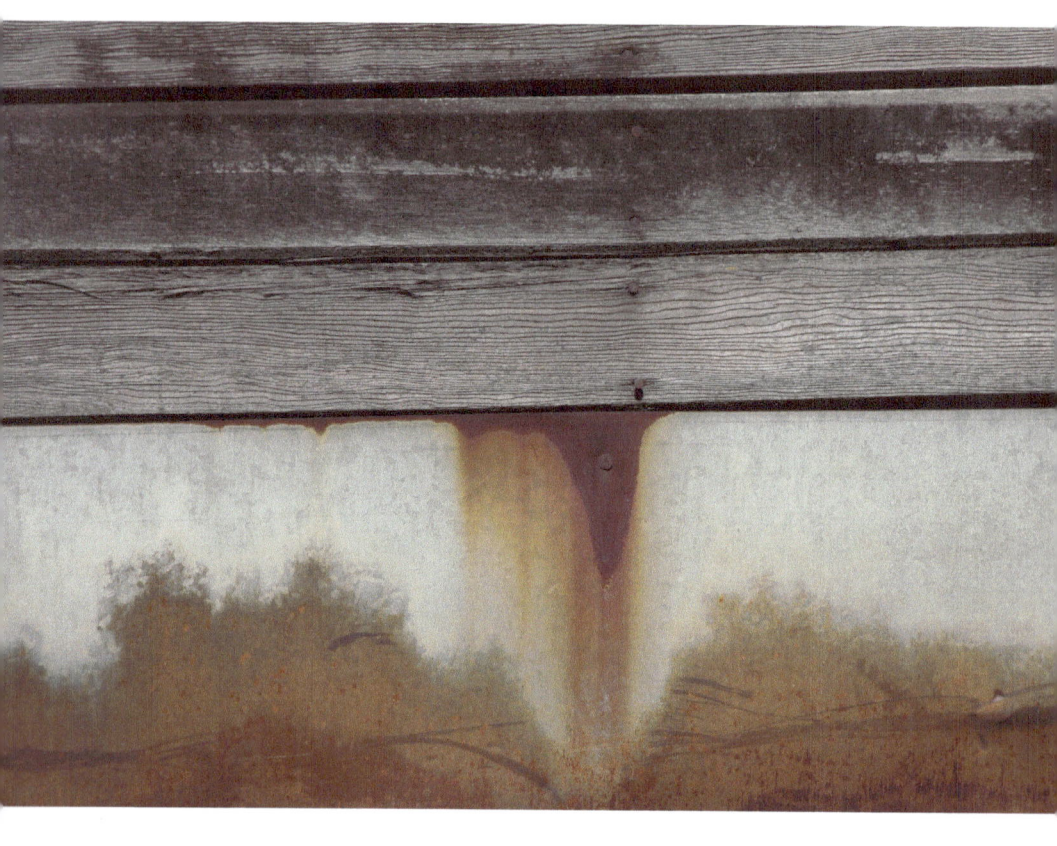

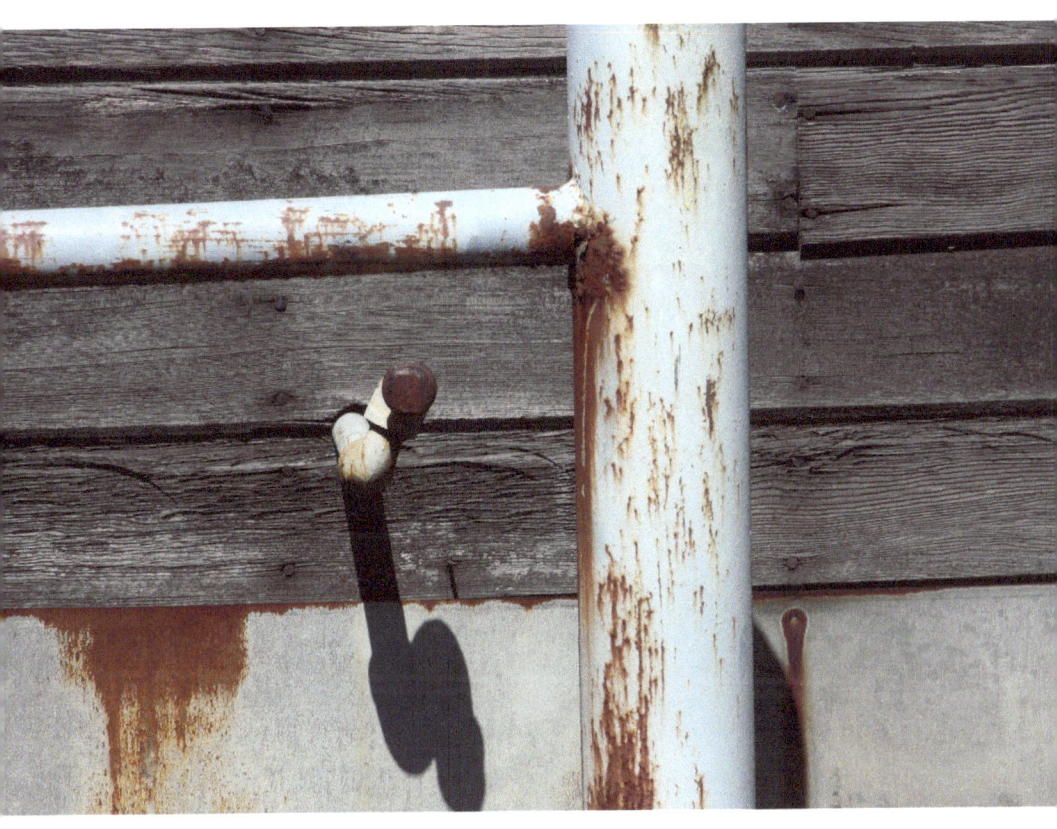

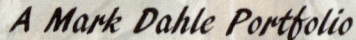

A Mark Dahle Portfolio

Amanda Gets A Pumpkin

(#1 in the series "Amanda Wanted A Miracle")

This Mark Dahle Portfolio includes a colorful painting, twenty-four beautiful industrial photographs from Beijing, Shangahi and Xian, and a story about a girl who wanted a miracle.

"Oh dear," said her grandmother. "You didn't want a pumpkin? Perhaps we'll have to try again."

This Mark Dahle Portfolio includes a colorful painting, twenty-six beautiful photographs from Detroit, and a story about a carpenter who made fine furniture from scraps.

The carpenter came across the twig one day while scouring the countryside for debris. He had already found a sheet of plastic, a broken piece of plywood and several rusty, bent nails. Those he knew he could use. But the twig? He could not imagine a use for it. Nevertheless, it caught his attention as he walked along the edge of a forest. He absentmindedly picked it up.

A Mark Dahle Portfolio

The Carpenter And The Twig

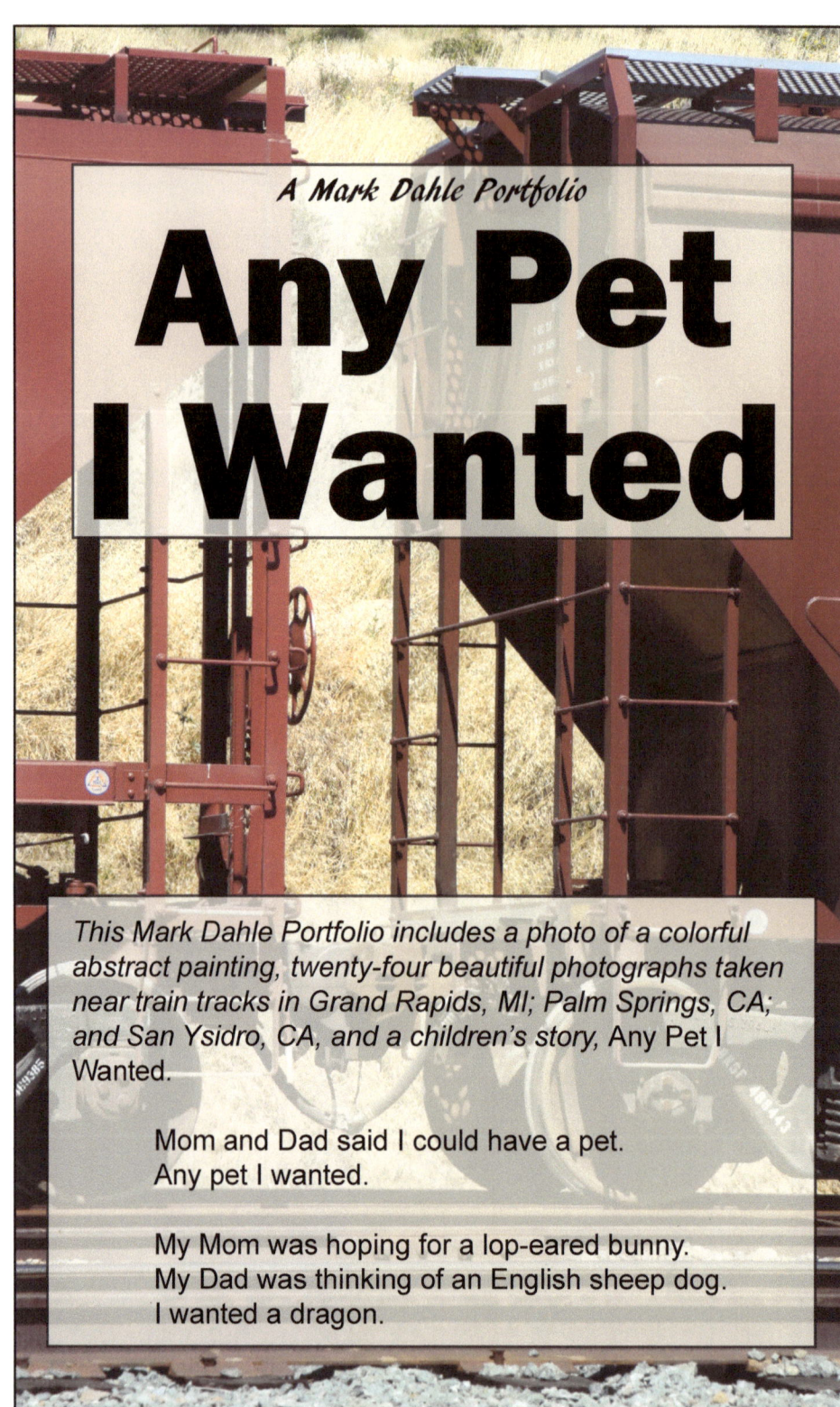

A Mark Dahle Portfolio

Any Pet I Wanted

This Mark Dahle Portfolio includes a photo of a colorful abstract painting, twenty-four beautiful photographs taken near train tracks in Grand Rapids, MI; Palm Springs, CA; and San Ysidro, CA, and a children's story, Any Pet I Wanted.

Mom and Dad said I could have a pet.
Any pet I wanted.

My Mom was hoping for a lop-eared bunny.
My Dad was thinking of an English sheep dog.
I wanted a dragon.

www.ingramcontent.com/pod-product-compliance
Lightning Source LLC
Chambersburg PA
CBHW040902180526
45159CB00001B/491